SENSORY PLAY

FOR TODDLERS AND PRESCHOOLERS

SENSORY PLAY
FOR TODDLERS AND PRESCHOOLERS

Easy Projects to Develop Fine Motor Skills,
Hand-Eye Coordination, and
Early Measurement Concepts

CASEY PATCH

Skyhorse Publishing

Skyhorse Publishing books may be purchased in bulk at special discounts for sales promotion, corporate gifts, fund-raising, or educational purposes. Special editions can also be created to specifications. For details, contact the Special Sales Department, Skyhorse Publishing, 307 West 36th Street, 11th Floor, New York, NY 10018 or info@skyhorsepublishing.com.

Skyhorse® and Skyhorse Publishing® are registered trademarks of Skyhorse Publishing, Inc.®, a Delaware corporation.

Visit our website at www.skyhorsepublishing.com.

10 9 8 7 6 5 4 3 2 1

Library of Congress Cataloging-in-Publication Data is available on file.

Cover design by Daniel Brount
Cover photo credit: Casey Patch

Print ISBN: 978-1-5107-5601-4

Printed in China

To Lilly, Elliot, Audrey—the world is your playground!

Contents

Introduction   viii

Chapter 1: Getting Started—What is
Sensory Play?   **1**
    Benefits of Sensory Play   2
    Tips and Tricks   4
    Sensory Play Staples   6

Chapter 2: Sensory Bases   **9**
    Rainbow Rice   11
    Rainbow Chickpeas   14
    Rainbow Spaghetti   17
    Cloud Dough   18
    Dirt Dough   21
    Edible Mud   22
    Sand Foam   25
    Chickpea Foam   27
    Oobleck   28
    Edible Water Beads   30
    Bubbly Soap Foam   33
    Water Tub   35
    No-Cook Play Dough   39

Chapter 3: Sensory Invitations   **43**
    Color Bath   44
    Bird Seed Pouring Tub   47
    Lemon Tray   48
    Flower Soup   51
    Play Dough Small Worlds   52

Lavender Sensory Tub   55
Frozen Water Beads   57
Frozen Building Blocks   61
Edible Ocean Small World   62
Sticky Wall   64
Wash the Pigs   67
Frozen Oobleck Blocks   71
Outdoor Kitchen   74
Jell-O Bug Rescue   77
Polenta Construction Tub   79
Frozen Nature Blocks   83
Fizzy Fish   85
Colorful Explosions   89

Chapter 4: Paint and Create   **93**
    Bubble Wrap Paintings   95
    Sensory Artwork   97
    Ice Painting   99
    Bath Paints   101
    Nature's Paintbrushes   103
    Spice Paints   105
    Seed Rolling   106
    Clay Sculptures   108
    Mirror Painting   110

Final Notes   113
About the Author   114
Index   116

Introduction

On a warm, sunny day, I opened the microwave and placed a mud pie inside. Embellished with dandelions and bark from the garden, it was the first tasty treat I had made for my imaginary bakery. I was about seven years old, and this moment will forever be etched in my memory and my heart.

Yes! We had an old microwave, bowls, and mixing spoons readily available in our sandpit to encourage loads of child-led play! I was fortunate enough to be raised by a mother who valued and cherished play. She so thoughtfully created play experiences for my brother, sisters, and me that allowed us to make connections and learn about the world around us through play.

I remember when my mother dyed the bath water blue and made us blue pasta for our dinner in an effort to engage our senses and create some magical memories while she was at it. Fast forward many years, I'm now a parent, and I think back to my childhood

and it gives me all the warm and fuzzy feelings! And THAT is what it's all about—using sensory play to connect with our little ones while also giving them a wonderful foundation to build future scientific and world-knowledge upon.

Sensory play allows our little learners to make connections as they explore the world around them using their senses of sight, smell, taste, sound, and touch. It's the beginning of a lifelong journey of scientific understanding! You've probably witnessed the wonder and awe on your child's face as they experience something new. When

my daughter started solids, I remember the grin that took over her entire face whenever we gave her a piece of mango. She was so excited to squash it between her fingers and smoosh it into her mouth. But her favorite part? Throwing it straight onto the floor. It was a bit of an experiment and one of the ways she explored cause and effect as a baby.

In this book, I hope you find lots of simple sensory play inspiration to support you during this magical time of your life as a parent or educator of little people.

Of course, there are many opportunities to explore and learn through our senses in our everyday experiences, like feeling the sand beneath our toes at the beach or running around outside on a rainy day! However, sometimes we all need and want a bit of extra motivation or support to bring more sensory play into our homes. Throughout this book, you're going to be armed with a multitude of tried and tested sensory play recipes and play ideas to inspire your playtime!

So, what are you waiting for? Let's get stuck into some sometimes-messy, often crazy, but always memorable sensory play with your little learners!

"Play is the way children discover themselves—starting with their fingers and toes and gradually including their whole body, their emotions and their minds."

—JOAN ALMON, US ALLIANCE FOR CHILDHOOD

Pictured right, Flower Soup, page 51.

CHAPTER 1

Getting Started—What is Sensory Play?

As I mentioned earlier, sensory play is any kind of play that allows our little learners to explore and play using any or all of their five senses of sight, taste, touch, smell, and sound. From birth, our little learners are exploring the world around them, making connections and strengthening the neural pathways to their brains. While they are surrounded by sensory stimulus during their day-to-day, we can also set up sensory play invitations or activities to further support their development and encourage open-ended, creative, messy play!

One of the most common misconceptions I hear about sensory play is that it's time-consuming and expensive, but that is simply not the case! Sensory play doesn't need to be fancy, and it certainly doesn't need to take you a lot of time to prepare. In fact, the best sensory play experiences are generally the ones we throw together quickly!

In general, most sensory play experiences include a base of some kind. This might be something like rainbow rice, dyed water, cooked spaghetti, or even play dough. The options are only limited by your imagination!

Before we move into the quick and easy sensory play ideas, let's first explore why sensory play is so beneficial, some quick tips to ensure your sensory play is successful, and my sensory play staples!

BENEFITS OF SENSORY PLAY

LIFE SKILLS

Your child can learn so much through play! As they scoop and pour sensory bases, they're developing their fine motor skills, hand-eye coordination, and early measurement concepts. As they learn to pour rice from one container to the next, they're fine-tuning those skills, which they'll use time and time again as they become older and begin helping in the kitchen, preparing their own snacks, and later learning to write.

ORAL LANGUAGE SKILLS

While your child explores a sensory tub or activity, they're developing their vocabulary and oral language as they talk about their play. You might like to facilitate this discussion by talking about things that are sticky, smelly, gooey, cold, warm, wet, loud, and quiet.

MEMORY MAKING

Sensory play isn't just about the educational benefits. It's also a wonderful way to strengthen the bond between you and your child and create some pretty magical memories of play! Sometimes we all struggle to put our devices away, but sensory play gives us an amazing opportunity to dedicate some time to play uninterrupted with our little ones.

QUICK AND EASY

Stop spending hours trawling the internet for ideas or spending more time setting up for play than your children actually play for! My tried and tested play ideas are designed to be quick and easy to implement without needing to spend a fortune on supplies or fancy toys. In fact, we often have one or two tubs set up and ready to grab whenever we need a quick and easy activity to reset those cranky pre-dinner moods!

HAVE FUN

There's no right or wrong way to do sensory play. It's all about the process and the exploration. Even if you think your child is doing it "wrong"—they're still going to be learning lots and, most importantly, having fun!

TIP:

Adding some tweezers or tongs to your sensory tub is a really easy way to encourage fine motor skill development and hand-eye coordination!

TIPS AND TRICKS

If you're just getting started with sensory play, you might be feeling a little overwhelmed. Here are some quick tips and tricks so that you can start enjoying simple sensory play with your little ones today!

PREPARE IN ADVANCE

Make sure you have everything you need on hand before you get started. Consider having simple sensory tubs set up that you can grab easily when you need a quick activity during those tricky witching hours!

DOCUMENT THE MEMORIES

Have a camera close by to capture some of the magic of sensory play. It's such a fun experience and special part of childhood so you don't want to miss out on capturing any funny moments like paint smeared all over your child's face!

CONTAIN THE MESS

Sensory play can get messy, so think about how you can contain the mess. A big, underbed storage container on top of an old bed sheet works wonders! The sheet will catch any spills and an underbed storage tub is big enough for little ones to sit inside. Sometimes I've been known to pop the kids in the bath tub or outside on the lawn just to contain the mess.

SUPERVISION IS KEY

Sensory play must be supervised. Do not leave your child unattended during any of the activities mentioned in this book. Be sure to use your best judgment before beginning any of the activities.

CONSIDER THE CLEAN UP

How will you clean up when you finish? Consider having a wet washcloth ready or keeping the activity set up in a tub that can be easily removed from your play area and tidied up safely.

KEEP IT SIMPLE, SILLY

Don't overthink it, and don't strive for perfection! Just jump in and create some special memories together. Sometimes we can try to be too fancy or elaborate, but simple is always the best!

SENSORY PLAY STAPLES

As I mentioned earlier, sensory play doesn't need to be fancy or expensive. In fact, you probably have everything you need to get started in your home already!

PANTRY STAPLES

Our pantry is the greatest source of sensory play fun! We use expired cereal with our digger toys; polenta as sand; and make edible dirt with cornstarch, cocoa powder, and oil. Food dyes are perfect for color baths and split peas make wonderful bases for sensory tubs! Many foods like coconut, custard, and Jell-O make fantastic edible bases for small-world play.

KITCHEN UTENSILS

Measuring cups, spoons, bowls, ladles, scoops, medicine syringes, funnels, and whisks all make wonderful additions to sensory tubs. And the best part? They all contribute to early measurement understandings while being explored with a sensory base like rainbow rice or uncooked pasta.

SENSORY TUB

You don't need to spend a lot of money on expensive sensory tables. Any old tub or tray will do! I like to use a big underbed storage tub with a sheet underneath to catch any spills. When picking a tub for sensory play, I just like to make sure it has a bit of a lip on the side to help catch spills and contain our sensory bases.

ANIMAL FIGURINES

We love to use animals in our small-world play. Not only is it a really simple and effective way to build oral language skills and vocabulary, but it's also a really fun way to encourage creative play with our little learners. You can pick these up at your local zoo or aquarium fairly cheaply!

TIP:

Recycled materials like egg cartons, cardboard tubes, and empty jars are a wonderful addition to your sensory play toolkit. Toddlers will love using a funnel to pour sensory bases into an old egg carton or recycled baby food jars!

CHAPTER 2

Sensory Bases

Every sensory tub starts with a simple sensory base! While all these bases will encourage your little learner to dive in hands first, many are also taste-safe for curious little explorers.

The sensory bases featured in this chapter are all wonderful stand-alone sensory play activities. However, you can extend their life by adding extra props like animal figurines to create exciting small worlds or containers to practice scooping and pouring. The only limit is your imagination!

Throughout this chapter, you'll find thirteen of our favorite tried and tested sensory base recipes, each using ingredients you already have in your pantry. Turn a can of chickpeas into a delightful, foamy sensory tub and learn how to color your own rainbow rice in minutes.

RAINBOW RICE

Rainbow rice is a staple sensory base in our home! While your little learners explore a tub of rainbow rice, they can begin to build early mathematical language such as *full*, *empty*, *heavy*, *light*, *tall*, and *wide*. They will also develop their hand-eye coordination as they pour and transfer the rice from container to container.

WHAT YOU'LL NEED:
- 1 cup uncooked rice (long grain)
- 1 tablespoon vinegar
- Liquid food dyes
- Sandwich bags
- Measuring cups and spoons
- Baking tray
- Shallow tub for play
- Kitchen utensils such as measuring cups, bowls, spoons, and funnels

THE PROCESS:
Add a cup of uncooked rice to a sandwich bag and then add a tablespoon of vinegar and several drops of your chosen food dye. The vinegar helps disperse the color evenly!

Continued on page 13

Seal the bag and shake it around, coating the rice with your chosen color. This is a great way to get your children involved—they'll love shaking the bag around and smooshing the rice together between their fingers. If your rice isn't bright enough, you can add more dye until you're happy with the vibrancy.

Once the rice has been coated, spread it out onto a baking tray and leave it in the sun to dry. You can repeat this process for each color of the rainbow.

Rainbow rice can be used over and over for many years! Once you're finished, just pop it in a container with an airtight seal and it will keep without issue!

EXTEND IT

Create a blue discovery tub by dying some rice blue and then collecting different objects from around the house to place inside. You can add blue cups, measuring spoons, balls, buttons, pom-poms, popsicle sticks, blocks, and funnels. This is a really simple and exciting way to talk about colors with your child!

Consider making rainbow rice for different occasions. I like to dye our rice red and green at Christmas time and then add a few drops of peppermint essence to ignite the sense of smell as we play!

RAINBOW CHICKPEAS

Not only do rainbow chickpeas look amazing, but they also make the most wonderful sound when used with aluminum bowls, whisks, and cups! You can add them straight to a tub without dying them or you can color them with acrylic paints!

WHAT YOU'LL NEED:
- Packet of uncooked chickpeas
- Sandwich bags
- Acrylic paints
- Parchment paper
- Baking tray
- Shallow tub for play

THE PROCESS:

Add the chickpeas to a sandwich bag—you'll need a sandwich bag for each color. Squirt some acrylic paint into the bag using approximately one teaspoon per two handfuls of chickpeas.

Seal the bag and shake it around, coating the paint all over the chickpeas. Lay the chickpeas out on some parchment paper to dry. You may need to shake the tray around every five minutes or so to stop the chickpeas from drying together.

Once dry, you can add your chickpeas to a tub with some aluminum kitchen bowls, cups, and utensils!

EXTEND IT

Estimate and then count how many spoons it takes to fill your bowl with chickpeas! This is a great way to develop early mathematical concepts and skills while playing.

RAINBOW SPAGHETTI

While your little learner explores a tub of rainbow spaghetti, they're working their hand-eye coordination and their fine motor skills. This is also a wonderful way to develop their pincer grip, which will later help them when they start to write!

WHAT YOU'LL NEED:
- Uncooked spaghetti
- Pot of water
- Liquid food dyes
- Shallow tub for play

THE PROCESS:
Cook a packet of spaghetti on the stove as you would normally, adding approximately two tablespoons of colored food dye to the water as it cooks. Drain the spaghetti as usual and then run it under cold water until it is cool enough to touch.

Add the colored spaghetti to a tub for your little learner to explore! You might like to dye a selection of colors to create the ultimate rainbow sensory tub.

Sometimes the spaghetti can get a little sticky, but if you run it through some cold water again, it should start to soften up a bit more.

EXTEND IT
We like to make an ocean small-world tray using blue spaghetti, aquarium plants, and some animal figurines! This is a great way to encourage creativity, imaginative play, and develop oral language skills and vocabulary.

Sometimes we like to add a pair of scissors to our spaghetti tub so our little learners can practice their cutting skills!

CLOUD DOUGH

Cloud dough is such an easy, quick recipe that your little learners can even help you make! It's very similar in texture to damp sand at the beach in that it can be powdery like flour but can also be shaped and molded together. It also makes a wonderful base for small-world play.

WHAT YOU'LL NEED:
- 4 cups plain flour
- ½ cup canola/vegetable oil
- Liquid food dyes (optional)
- Shallow tub for play

THE PROCESS:

Have your little learner mix the flour with the oil to create your cloud dough. The quantities above can be doubled for a bigger batch!

Pour the cloud dough into a shallow tub with some spoons and containers for your little learner to explore, mold, and build.

You can also color your cloud dough by dropping some food dye into the oil before you mix it together!

EXTEND IT

Add some creepy crawly toys, branches, and pebbles from the garden to turn your cloud dough into an inviting small world!

DIRT DOUGH

While real dirt provides invaluable sensory input, sometimes it's just not practical to head outside to play. We like to alter our cloud dough recipe to make our very own taste-safe dirt dough, which is perfect for small-world play!

WHAT YOU'LL NEED:
- 3 cups plain flour
- 1 cup cocoa powder
- ½ cup canola/vegetable oil
- Shallow tub for play

THE PROCESS:
Mix the flour and cocoa powder together. This is a great way to get your little learner involved and using big arm movements! Add the oil and mix together well.

Pour the dirt dough into a shallow tub ready for your little learner to explore.

Your dirt dough should keep in a sealed container for several weeks. In fact, one of my batches is still going strong after a year of play!

EXTEND IT
We like to add our little construction vehicles to a tub of dirt dough! You could add some small pebbles or rocks as well.

EDIBLE MUD

All children love to play in mud, but sometimes it can be hard to find in your suburban backyard. The next best thing is homemade mud, which is also edible! You can also build early language skills by reciting rhymes and stories about pigs in mud.

WHAT YOU'LL NEED:
- 3 cups plain flour
- 1 cup cocoa powder
- 2 cups water
- Shallow tub for play

THE PROCESS:
Mix the flour and cocoa powder together. This is a great way to get your little learner involved! Add the water, and mix together well. For a thicker mud, you can use less water.

Pour the edible mud into a tub ready for your little learner to explore!

Alternatively, you can make a batch of chocolate pudding, which is even tastier for younger toddlers.

EXTEND IT

For an extra sensory element, add some cooked spaghetti "worms" for your little learner to find in the mud! Add a pair of tongs to pick up the worms to make it a little bit trickier.

In the past, we've added some little pigs to our edible mud! By adding a dish of bubbly water, our little learners were able to wash off their pigs when they had finished playing.

SAND FOAM

This is a wonderful activity for exploring different textures! In fact, I find it really hard not to get my hands in on this one. Your little learner will love helping mix the ingredients together for this recipe.

WHAT YOU'LL NEED:

- Shaving cream
- Sand
- Shallow tub for play

THE PROCESS:

Simply place some sand in a tray and then invite your little learner to spray some shaving cream on top. The proportions are totally up to you!

Your little learner can use their hands to mix the two ingredients together. This is a really fun way for young children to begin exploring cause and effect as they play. They'll notice how the two ingredients mix together to create a new texture that is really exciting to explore.

EXTEND IT

Talk about how the different ingredients feel as you mix them together. Can your little learner think of anything else that feels grainy or fluffy?

Place some creepy crawly toys in the sand foam for an added element of fun!

CHICKPEA FOAM

Your little learner will love exploring this fluffy sensory base! And the best part? It's totally taste-safe for your more curious littles!

WHAT YOU'LL NEED:
- 1 (15-ounce) can chickpeas
- 1 tablespoon Cream of Tartar
- Liquid food dyes
- Electric beater
- Shallow tub for play

THE PROCESS:
Strain the liquid from a can of chickpeas into a bowl. Put the leftover chickpeas aside to use in your cooking later.

Add a tablespoon of cream of tartar (it helps the foam keep its shape) and then beat with an electric mixer until stiff peaks form. Pour the chickpea foam into a shallow tub ready for your little learner to explore!

You might like to add a few drops of food dye to color your chickpea foam, as well. You could even split the foam into three different bowls and gently fold through the coloring to make a batch of several different colors.

EXTEND IT
Add some silicone cupcake molds, spoons, sprinkles, and candles so your little learner can make their own chickpea foam cupcakes!

OOBLECK

Oobleck is something I have very fond memories of making as a child, so I just know your little learners are going to love it too! Oobleck is a non-Newtonian substance, meaning it's a liquid when poured and a solid when a force is acting upon it. Oobleck play is a wonderful way to begin exploring scientific concepts such as liquids, solids, forces, and motion.

WHAT YOU'LL NEED:

- 1 cup cornstarch
- ½ cup water
- Food dye
- Bowl
- Shallow tub for play

THE PROCESS:

Add the cornstarch to a bowl and slowly pour in the water, mixing as you go. It will become tougher to mix as you add more of the water. It should be easy to pick up and roll into a ball but will then melt away in your hands once you stop moving the substance in your hands.

You can leave your Oobleck plain, or you can add some food dye to the water before you begin mixing. Sometimes we like to add a few drops to the surface of the Oobleck once we add it to a tray.

If your Oobleck is too runny, slowly add more cornstarch until you reach the desired consistency. If you leave it to set for a while, you can add a splash of water to make it squashy again!

EXTEND IT

Make your Oobleck even more exciting by adding some glitter! You could also try mixing two different colors together.

Watch what happens when you drip the Oobleck into a colander or over a cooling rack. Experiment with different containers!

EDIBLE WATER BEADS

Edible sensory tubs are a wonderful way to encourage our little learners to explore the sense of taste during their play! Couscous Pearls can be found in a box at your local supermarket and make the perfect taste-safe base for a sensory tub.

WHAT YOU'LL NEED:
- Couscous Pearls
- Water in a pot
- Food dyes
- Shallow tub for play
- Cups and spoons

THE PROCESS:
To cook the Couscous Pearls, simply follow the instructions on the back of the packet or box. You can add a splash of food dye to the water as it cooks to easily color them.

Add the colored Couscous Pearls to a shallow tub with some cups and spoons, but don't be surprised when your little learner dives in hands first to explore the inviting texture.

And the best part about this sensory tub? The Couscous Pearls are totally taste-safe for children that still like to mouth things as they play.

EXTEND IT

Experiment with freezing the Couscous Pearls into some ice cube trays! Can you make different colored Couscous Pearl ice cubes?

BUBBLY SOAP FOAM

This bubbly, soapy sensory tub is perfect for warmer weather! It also makes a wonderful base for soapy potions in your outdoor play space.

WHAT YOU'LL NEED:

- 2 tablespoons bubble bath liquid
- ½ cup water
- Food dyes
- Electric beater
- Shallow tub for play

THE PROCESS:

Add the bubble bath liquid to a bowl and top with the water. Add a few drops of food dye and mix to combine. Using an electric beater, beat the mixture until stiff peaks form. Scoop the bubbly soap foam into a shallow tub ready to explore!

You can make one color of soap foam to explore or you can make several batches, all with different colors. Add them one by one to a tub ready for your little learner to scoop and mix!

EXTEND IT

Add some wooden spoons to encourage your little learner to use big arm movements to mix the bubbly soap foam together! This is a wonderful way to strengthen their arm muscles and upper body strength.

WATER TUB

All children love to play in water. Not only does it fulfill their need to explore water movement, but it also allows them to develop their pouring and transferring skills, building important mathematical understandings while they play.

WHAT YOU'LL NEED:
- Water
- Large tub
- Cups and spoons
- Watering cans

Continued on page 37

THE PROCESS:

Fill a large tub with water and place it on a table at the upper-stomach height of your little learner. Young children are top-heavy, so it's important that the tub is placed at the right height so they don't topple over into the tub. As always, close supervision is the key.

Add containers of different sizes to the water and invite your little learner to explore! You could add things like watering cans, spinning wheels, squirt/spray bottles, and containers with holes.

You might even like to add some squirt/spray bottles filled with water and colored with different food dyes. Your little learner will love exploring how the colors mix together to make new colors!

EXTEND IT

Color the water with blue food dye and add some little yellow rubber ducks! Read a book about ducks and enjoy splashing in the water on a warm summer day.

You might even like to pick a color theme and add different bowls, containers, and loose parts like pom-poms and plastic toys that match the color scheme! This is a wonderful way to explore colors with your little learner.

NO-COOK PLAY DOUGH

Play dough is one of the sensory play activities that we *always* have on hand! It's perfect for keeping busy hands occupied when you go out for dinner or travel by plane. Play dough is also a great way to begin exploring early measurement skills and the ability to follow a simple recipe.

WHAT YOU'LL NEED:

- 1 cup plain flour
- ½ cup salt
- 1 tablespoon Cream of Tartar
- 1 tablespoon canola/vegetable oil
- 1 cup boiling water

Continued on page 41

THE PROCESS:

Add all the dry ingredients to a bowl and mix with a wooden spoon. Slowly pour in the boiling water and oil, then mix gently with a wooden spoon.

Empty the mix onto a chopping board and knead until it comes together. If it's a little wet, add some more flour, and if it's a little dry, add some more water.

You can add some food dye or cooking essences either to the water or at the end to knead through. Sometimes we like to leave our play dough plain for a more natural sensory base. You can store your play dough in an airtight container or bag for several weeks.

We like to add some crafty loose parts to a tray with our play dough to encourage lots of creative play! Things like pebbles, buttons, popsicle sticks, and googly eyes all make wonderful additions to your play dough play.

EXTEND IT

Dye your play dough brown and pretend it is dirt! Add some small plastic plant pots and some artificial flowers for your little learner to create their own floral arrangements.

CHAPTER 3

Sensory Invitations

One of my favorite features of sensory play is that it's totally open-ended. The focus is on the *exploration* rather than a completed project or set of steps that must be followed. This means that your little learner can take control and explore the invitation or activity in a way that suits their own needs at the time.

Throughout this chapter, I'll share some of our favorite sensory invitations, which I use over and over to both excite and engage my little learners in meaningful play. You'll learn how to set up a play dough small world to encourage hours of independent, creative play and how to use natural loose parts to create inviting frozen ice blocks!

COLOR BATH

Color baths are a wonderful way to introduce your little learner to colors! They can also develop their gross motor skills as they kick and splash in the water.

WHAT YOU'LL NEED:
- Bath
- Liquid food dyes
- Colored loose parts from around the house

THE PROCESS:
Simply pick a color and go on a color hunt around the house! Find different items such as colored cups, spoons, balls, bath toys, pom-poms, and teething toys.

Add a few drops of food dye to the water as you fill the bath. I haven't experienced the dye coloring our bath or children—just a few drops is all you need!

You could try having a different color bath every night throughout the week! They are such an exciting, tactile experience for young children.

EXTEND IT

Sometimes my mother would have a color theme for the whole day! We'd have green milk for breakfast, green pasta at dinner time, followed by a green bath before bed. It was the best fun and I still have fond memories of our themed color days even as an adult!

BIRD SEED POURING TUB

Bird seed is a fantastic, affordable base for sensory play! Coupled with some wooden bowls and mixing spoons, it makes for a very inviting sensory base to practice pouring and scooping skills while developing hand-eye coordination.

WHAT YOU'LL NEED:
- Packet of bird seed
- Wooden bowls
- Wooden mixing spoons
- Shallow tub for play

THE PROCESS:
Pour a packet of bird seed into a shallow tub, and add some small wooden or bamboo bowls and cups. Your little learner will love pouring the seed from bowl to bowl and using wooden utensils to mix and scoop the seed.

You might even like to add some funnels or scoops so your little learner can further develop their fine motor skills as they explore and play!

EXTEND IT
Bird seed makes a fantastic base for a bird-themed small-world tray! Add some twigs, artificial bird nests, and make some little eggs from clay. Your little learner will love creating imaginative play scenes with this sensory tub!

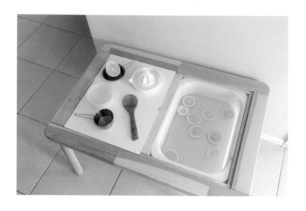 

LEMON TRAY

Sensory play is all about igniting the senses, and this lemon tray does just that! Not only can your little learner taste and smell the lemons as they play, but they'll also love exploring with their hands and cooking utensils, too!

WHAT YOU'LL NEED:
- Shallow tub for play
- Water
- Yellow food dye
- Lemon slices
- Cooking utensils

THE PROCESS:
Slice some lemons to create lemon rounds to add to your sensory tub. Fill your tub with water, and add a splash of yellow food dye to color the water. You could add a dash of lemon essence to the water, as well, for a stronger lemon scent as your little learner plays.

Add your lemon slices and some cooking utensils like wooden spoons, tongs, whisks, and aluminum bowls for your little learner to mix together!

You might like to add some frozen ice cubes or even some yellow flower petals to add an extra sensory element to this tub!

EXTEND IT

Create a lemonade stand dramatic play space by adding whole lemons, a lemon juicer, a ladle, reusable cups, and some straws. This is a great opportunity to develop oral language skills and creativity through play!

FLOWER SOUP

Flowers are a wonderful addition to your sensory play toolkit! Whether they're fresh from the garden or purchased from the Farmer's Market, they are an excellent sensory stimulus during playtime!

WHAT YOU'LL NEED:
- Fresh flowers
- Kitchen utensils
- Bowls and containers
- Shallow tub for play
- Glitter and food dyes (optional)

THE PROCESS:
Have your little learner help cut flowers off their stems and add them to a bowl. Fill the tub with water and add the fresh flowers to the water. You can add a splash of food dye to color the water if you like!

Invite your little learner to mix up some flower soups or potions using wooden spoons, ladles, bowls, and even some glitter shakers if you're feeling brave!

EXTEND IT
When you're finished with the flowers, you could add them to a tub of Oobleck or even to a fresh batch of play dough!

PLAY DOUGH SMALL WORLDS

Not only is play dough a wonderful way to strengthen the small muscles in our fingers, it's also a wonderful sensory base for small-world play! Your little learner can begin developing vocabulary, oral language skills, and creative thinking as they play, too.

WHAT YOU'LL NEED:
- Fresh batch of play dough (see recipe on page 39)
- Animal figurines
- Aquarium plants or artificial plants
- Pebbles and rocks from the garden
- Branches and sticks from the garden
- Shells and coral from the beach

THE PROCESS:
Decide on a theme and collect your materials! When we make an ocean-themed small world, we dye our play dough blue or add some sand to natural play dough. Next, we add some loose parts like shells, coral, and driftwood before adding our animal figurines

For a garden small world, we add some green or brown coloring to our play dough and collect loose parts from the garden like small pebbles, branches, fallen leaves, and fresh flowers. Our little creepy crawly animals that we purchased from our local zoo complete the small world!

You can present your small world in a sectioned tray so that your little learner can construct their own play! This is a wonderful way to support their creativity and give them ownership over their play.

EXTEND IT

Take photos of the animals you're going to use in your small world and print them off on small cards. Your little learner can then match their animal toys to the picture cards! This is a great way to develop their vocabulary and sorting skills.

LAVENDER SENSORY TUB

Lavender is well known for its calming affects, so it's one of my favorite scents to add to our sensory play! Our first batch of lavender sensory rice is still going strong one year later.

WHAT YOU'LL NEED:
- 2 cups uncooked long-grain rice
- 1 tablespoon vinegar
- Lavender essential oil
- Purple food dye
- Sandwich bag
- Baking tray
- Dried lavender

Continued on page 56

THE PROCESS:

Add the uncooked rice to a sandwich bag with a tablespoon of vinegar. You can add a few drops of lavender essential oil and the purple food dye at this stage, too. If you don't have purple, add blue and red food dye at a ratio of 3:1 to get a soft purple color.

Next, seal the bag and shake it around, coating the rice with the food dye. This is a great way to get your little learner involved!

Next, you can spread your rice out onto a baking tray and leave it in the sun to dry. When your rice dries, you can add some dried lavender! Add some scoops and little wooden bowls for the ultimate calming sensory tub!

EXTEND IT

What other cooking essences could you use with your rainbow rice? You could make some red and green peppermint scented rice at Christmas time or some lemon scented rice for a fresh, spring-themed sensory tub!

FROZEN WATER BEADS

Water Beads are probably one of the most popular sensory play items money can buy right now, and if you've ever played with them, it's easy to see why! These frozen water beads will enable your little learner to develop an understanding of temperature, heating, cooling, and changes to matter as they melt and disintegrate!

WHAT YOU'LL NEED:
- Water Beads (already made)
- Ice cube trays (we love sphere-shaped trays!)
- Water
- Shallow tub for play
- Spray bottle with warm water

Continued on page 59

THE PROCESS:

Make a batch of Water Beads by following the instructions on the packet. Next, fill your ice cube trays with water beads and then top with water. It's important that you fully swell the beads before adding them to the ice cube trays.

Once frozen, add them to a tub with some warm water in a spray bottle, and you're set! Invite your little learner to use a spray bottle to melt the water bead ice cubes. Watch to see what happens to the water beads as the ice melts away.

EXTEND IT

Give your child a small hammer so they can crack and hammer the frozen water bead ice cubes! This is a great activity for a warm, sunny day!

FROZEN BUILDING BLOCKS

Add a sensory element to your construction play by freezing water into cube shapes! You can create lots of different colors and explore color mixing as the blocks melt, as well.

WHAT YOU'LL NEED:
- Silicone ice cube tray
- Water
- Liquid food dyes
- Shallow tub for play

THE PROCESS:
Fill a measuring cup with water and add a splash of food dye to color the water. Pour it into the ice cube tray and set in the freezer overnight. Square or brick-shaped ice cube trays are perfect because they will allow your little learners to build them up into towers once frozen!

Twist the frozen ice cube blocks out into a shallow tub ready for your child to build with.

You might like to make lots of different shapes and colors or even just choose two primary colors like red and blue so that your little learner can explore color mixing as they melt.

EXTEND IT
How tall can you make your ice cube tower? Talk about how we can make estimations and then count to see how many blocks they can actually stack! Was their estimation right?

EDIBLE OCEAN SMALL WORLD

Explore different tastes, textures, and smells with this simple sensory small-world tub. This is perfect for children who like to taste, and it's a wonderful, multi-sensory experience for children big and small!

WHAT YOU'LL NEED:
- Shallow tub for play
- Blue Jell-O
- Shredded coconut
- Yellow food dye
- Ocean animals and toys

THE PROCESS:
First, you'll need to prepare the Jell-O as per the packet instructions. Once set, use a spoon to loosely cut the Jell-O into smaller chunks and place them into one end of your sensory tub.

Next, make the coconut sand by mixing some yellow food dye into the shredded coconut. Add it to the other side of your tub.

Finally, add some ocean animals and toys to the tub, and it will be ready for your little learner to explore! Not only does it look inviting, but it's also a great way to encourage imaginative play during your sensory play activity *and* it's totally taste-safe for younger children, too.

EXTEND IT

Try using some green coconut and some chocolate pudding mud to make an edible farm small-world tub. Your little learner will love exploring and tasting while they play!

STICKY WALL

This is a great activity for encouraging creative play with your little learner! As they attach flowers and leaves from the garden to the sticky wall, they're developing their fine motor skills, hand-eye coordination, and problem-solving skills.

WHAT YOU'LL NEED:
- Clear adhesive contact
- Painter's tape
- Flowers, leaves, grass, and other loose parts from the garden

THE PROCESS:
Attach a sheet of adhesive contact to the wall or glass door using painter's tape, making sure that the sticky side is facing outward to your child.

Collect a variety of light loose parts from the garden. Look for things like interesting flowers, petals, leaves, and small sticks. Place them in a bowl or sectioned tray ready for your little learner to stick to the sticky wall.

EXTEND IT
Cut some different shapes out of colored paper. Your little learner can develop their color knowledge as they sort, create patterns, and make colorful collages using the shapes!

WASH THE PIGS

While this invitation to play might seem very simple and straightforward, it's always been a huge success in our home! All you need is a plastic pig toy, an old toothbrush, and some hand soap, and you're ready to play.

WHAT YOU'LL NEED:

- Plastic pig toy
- Toothbrush
- Foaming hand soap in a pump bottle
- Towel
- Jug of water
- Shallow tub for play

Continued on page 68

THE PROCESS:

Grab a bottle of foaming hand soap from the supermarket and set it up in a tub with a plastic pig, an old toothbrush, a jug of water, and a towel.

Invite your little learner to wash the pig with the foaming soap, using the toothbrush to scrub the pig clean. This is a fantastic way to develop fine motor skills and hand-eye coordination in an exciting sensory play experience!

Once your little learner has cleaned their pig, they can use the jug of water to carefully wash away the soapy suds and then use the towel to dry their pig. You'll be surprised at how many times your little learner will want to complete this process.

EXTEND IT

Print out an outline of a pig onto pink cardboard and invite your little learner to finger paint some "mud" onto their pig cutout using brown paints.

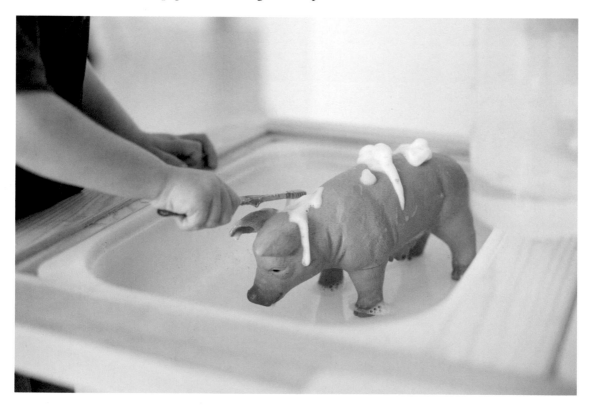

FROZEN OOBLECK BLOCKS

Oobleck is an exciting sensory experience, but creating a frozen element adds even more excitement to the activity! This sensory play tub is perfect for beginning to explore different states of matter with your little learner.

WHAT YOU'LL NEED:

- 1 cup cornstarch
- ½ cup water
- Liquid food dyes
- Silicone trays or molds
- Shallow tub for play

THE PROCESS:

Mix the cornstarch and water together in a bowl. It will be quite difficult to mix but you'll know you've got the right consistency when you can pick it up and roll it into a ball, but then it melts away in your hands when you stop rolling the substance.

If you'd like to make colored Oobleck, you can add a few drops of food dye to the water before you begin mixing.

Once mixed together, pour the mixture into silicone molds and freeze overnight. We get lots of our silicone molds online at places like eBay!

Continued on page 73

Once frozen, you can add the Oobleck blocks to a shallow tub for play. Sometimes we like to add a batch of fresh Oobleck to the base or just explore the frozen Oobleck blocks on their own.

EXTEND IT

Make a frozen artic small-world tray by adding a base of runny blue Oobleck to a shallow tray and then adding some larger blocks of frozen white Oobleck to represent large icebergs! You could freeze the white Oobleck in a long container or in smaller round containers. Add some orca whales and polar bears to your tray to create an exciting sensory small world!

OUTDOOR KITCHEN

Children love to play outside, so encouraging lots of creative, independent play outdoors in nature is a must! Creating an outdoor kitchen is so quick and easy and is sure to facilitate hours of imaginative play.

WHAT YOU'LL NEED:
- Kitchen utensils
- Metal bowls and trays
- Mortar and pestle
- Herbs and plants
- Scissors

THE PROCESS:

Add some old metal bowls, trays, and kitchen utensils (like wooden spoons, tongs, and ladles) to your outdoor play space. You could repurpose an old kitchen sink or simply add a tub of water to encourage lots of imaginative play!

Consider creating a little area in the garden full of herbs and plants that your little learner can use exclusively in their outdoor kitchen to make mud pies, mud cakes, and soups.

Sometimes we even add colored water (food dyes mixed into a squirt/spray bottle) or slices of lemon and orange. A mortar and pestle is also a wonderful addition to any outdoor kitchen.

EXTEND IT

Have your little learner create their very own outdoor kitchen recipe book! Take photos of their creations and have them help you write out recipes that can be laminated and added to your outdoor play space.

JELL-O BUG RESCUE

While your little learner rescues bugs from Jell-O, they're beginning to use early problem-solving skills. This activity is also a great way to explore sight, taste, touch, and smell!

WHAT YOU'LL NEED:
- Jell-O packet from the supermarket
- Jell-O molds
- Creepy crawly toys
- Spoon or tongs

Continued on page 78

THE PROCESS:

Follow the instructions on a packet of Jell-O to make a batch of green Jell-O. Fill each mold one-third of the way and place in the fridge to set. After a few hours, you can add a creepy crawly toy to each mold and top with more Jell-O. By setting one-third of the mold first, the creepy crawly won't sink to the bottom of the mold.

Once completely set, pop the Jell-O out onto a tray. Provide your little learner with spoons or tongs and invite them to "rescue" the bugs from the Jell-O.

The cool, wobbly texture of the Jell-O is really interesting, but it also tastes yummy!

EXTEND IT

Freeze smaller objects like pom-poms, blocks, or buttons into a large, flat tray of Jell-O. Invite your little learner to use tongs to rescue the objects. This is a really fun and easy way to work on their fine motor skills! Just remember to set the Jell-O in two stages so the pom-poms don't float to the top while setting.

POLENTA CONSTRUCTION TUB

Polenta makes such an inviting sensory base for small-world play, and we love to use it for a construction-themed small-world tray! Pair it with your child's favorite construction picture book for an inviting sensory small-world experience.

WHAT YOU'LL NEED:
- Shallow tub for play
- Packet of polenta
- Construction vehicles
- Natural loose parts

Continued on page 81

Continued on page 81

THE PROCESS:

Pour a packet of polenta into a shallow sensory tub, and then add some natural loose parts like branches and stones you can collect from your garden.

Add some of your child's favorite construction vehicles! The polenta is also taste-safe, so this tub would be perfect for younger children who like to taste while they explore and play.

EXTEND IT

We love using cereal as a base for small-world play so things like Rice Krispies and Chex make a wonderful sensory base for construction-themed small worlds!

FROZEN NATURE BLOCKS

Ice play is perfect for the warmer summer months! You can hide all sorts of objects inside ice, ready for your little learner to excavate!

WHAT YOU'LL NEED:

- Small cups, containers, or ice cube trays
- Natural loose parts from the garden
- Water
- Pipettes with warm water
- Shallow tub for play

Continued on page 84

THE PROCESS:

Find some small cups and containers or even larger ice cube trays to hide objects inside.

Collect some fresh flowers and leaves from the garden and add them to a cup. Half fill the cups with water and place in the freezer for approximately six hours. You will likely find that the flowers will float to the top of the water and freeze there, so by only half filling the cup, you can top it up with more water and freeze for another six hours! This way the flowers will be frozen in the middle of the ice block.

You can experiment with freezing the nature treasures in a large plastic container, round cake pans, round ice cube trays, or in silicone cupcake trays! However, the smaller the container, the faster it will be for your child to melt and free the flowers hidden inside.

Once frozen, you can pop your ice blocks into a shallow tub. You might like to invite your little learner to use a pipette to squirt warm water onto the ice blocks to melt them or simply add the ice blocks to a shallow tub of warm water.

EXTEND IT

What other small items could you freeze inside your ice blocks? We've added small dinosaur figurines and pom-poms to our frozen ice blocks before!

FIZZY FISH

Who doesn't love a fizzy science experiment? This activity is great for exploring simple color mixing and cause and effect!

WHAT YOU'LL NEED:
- 2 cups baking soda
- Water
- Food dyes
- Silicone fish molds
- 3 cups vinegar
- Shallow tub for play

THE PROCESS:
Add the baking soda to a bowl, and slowly mix in the water until you get a thick paste consistency. You can also add a few drops of food dye to color the paste. Pour the paste into fish-shaped silicone molds and place them into the freezer overnight.

Once the fish have set, you're ready to explore! Add some vinegar to a shallow tub and have your little learner explore what happens when they drop a fish into the vinegar tray!

By creating different-colored fish (yellow, green, and blue) your little learner can also begin to explore color mixing as the fish fizz and the colors mix together.

EXTEND IT

Rather than dropping the fish into the vinegar tray, you could add vinegar to a spray bottle so your little learner can squirt it onto the fish instead. They could even use pipettes to slowly drop vinegar onto the fish while developing their fine motor skills.

COLORFUL EXPLOSIONS

Begin exploring cause and effect with this fun science experiment! Your little learner will love seeing what secret colors are hidden beneath.

WHAT YOU'LL NEED:

- Food dye
- Baking soda
- Vinegar in a spray bottle OR a cup with a pipette
- A muffin tray, sectioned trays, or small bowls/cups
- Large tray to catch spills

Continued on page 91

THE PROCESS:

Add a few drops of food dye to the bottom of a cup or bowl or into the cups of a muffin tray. Cover the food dye with a generous amount of baking soda (the more the better) until the colors can't be seen anymore.

Give your little learner a spray bottle filled with vinegar or a cup with a pipette. Invite them to pour or squeeze the vinegar onto the baking soda to see what surprise color erupts from underneath!

This activity can get a little messy, so make sure you have the cups or muffin tray sitting on a larger tray or underbed storage container so you can catch the inevitable spills.

EXTEND IT

Use this activity to explore color mixing by adding just two cups—one with yellow food dye and the other with red food dye—so your little learner can explore how the two colors mix together on the tray to make orange.

CHAPTER 4

Paint and Create

Not only can sensory play support our little learners to build a solid foundation for scientific understandings, but it's also a wonderful way to begin encouraging creativity and exploring process-based art techniques.

Throughout this chapter, you'll learn how to set up simple art invitations that will encourage your little learner to explore different art mediums and processes through open-ended creative play experiences.

Your little learner will explore color and textures in their garden by using natural loose parts to create their own paintbrushes. You'll also be left with some beautiful memories and artworks to display in your learning space!

BUBBLE WRAP PAINTING

This art activity involves your little learner exploring paint on a new texture! Children of all ages will love finger painting and feeling the bumps beneath their fingers.

WHAT YOU'LL NEED:
- Bubble wrap
- Tape
- Nontoxic paints
- Tray
- Brushes and rollers
- Sheet of paper

Continued on page 96

THE PROCESS:

Cut a large piece of bubble wrap and tape it down onto your art table or a large piece of cardboard box that can be placed down on the grass outside. Add some rollers and paintbrushes to the table with a tray of paint. I like to use different tones of the same color, so we don't end up with a brown mess at the end.

Your little learner can use the brushes to paint the bubble wrap, which is a really fun, new texture to work with. They may even end up using their fingers and hands to really get into the sensory experience!

Once they're finished, they can make a print of their artwork by placing a piece of paper directly on top of their art and using their hands to press down onto the bubble wrap. When they lift their paper away, they'll be left with a print of their creation.

EXTEND IT

Cut their finished printed artwork into lots of smaller shapes. Your little learner can use those cut-out shapes to collage different pictures!

SENSORY ARTWORK

Children should be exposed to lots of opportunities to explore and create without any constraints. This is how they develop their confidence and creativity. Sensory artworks are a wonderful way to encourage our little learners to create!

WHAT YOU'LL NEED:
- An old cardboard box
- Nontoxic paints
- Brushes
- Craft glue
- Loose parts

THE PROCESS:
Invite your little learner to choose a color theme for their artwork. Help them paint a large piece of cardboard cut from the side of a cardboard box. I like to offer our little learners lots of different tones of one particular color, or even one color with some white and black paint, so they can create their own tonal variations. They love mixing and creating with their hands especially!

Continued on page 98

Your little learner can then glue various loose parts to their artwork! We added lots of different green loose parts to a tray for our little learners to choose from. Things like crepe paper, paper straws, buttons, glitter, and cupcake liners were all popular choices.

EXTEND IT

Your little learner can make nine different artworks by cutting out nine squares of cardboard. Each square can feature a different color. These would look beautiful displayed in your home or learning space!

ICE PAINTING

There's something magical about painting on ice! Your little learner will love creating artworks on a sheet of ice—and the best part? It can be washed off and ready to start over and over until the ice has all melted!

WHAT YOU'LL NEED:
- Plastic container
- Tray
- Watercolors
- Brush
- Water

THE PROCESS:

Add some water to a large plastic container and place it in the freezer overnight. When it's completely frozen, your little learner can begin to paint!

Set the ice block out on a tray with a brush, watercolors, and a cup of water. Your little learner can then use the ice block as a canvas for their painting! Their artwork will evolve and change as the ice melts, and they can wash it off under water to start again.

Continued on page 100

EXTEND IT

Make your own ice cube paints by squirting a teaspoon of nontoxic paint into each cube of an ice cube tray. Top with water, mix, and then add a popsicle stick to each cube. Place in the freezer to set. Once frozen, your little learner can use their frozen paint cubes as paintbrushes!

BATH PAINTS

This is a wonderful activity for those days when you want to do some sensory play but don't want to deal with the mess! Develop your little learner's creativity as they paint in the bath or shower.

WHAT YOU'LL NEED:
- Shaving cream OR moisturizer
- Liquid food dyes
- Ice cube tray

Continued on page 102

THE PROCESS:

Simply mix up some shaving cream or moisturizer and a drop of food dye into an ice cube tray. Mix the two ingredients well. Be sure not to use too much dye because it can stain your skin temporarily.

Place the tray in the bath tub or shower and invite your little learner to paint until their heart is content! When they're finished, show them how to wash the paints away with water.

EXTEND IT

Your little learner can experience color mixing by exploring how two bath paints mix together to create new colors! You can extend this activity by exploring with colored water outside in the garden by adding a few drops of food dye to some cups of water.

NATURE'S PAINTBRUSHES

There's nothing more magical than exploring the great outdoors with our little learners! So why not stop and collect some natural paintbrushes during your next nature walk? Keep an eye out for interesting shapes and textures that could be turned into paintbrushes!

WHAT YOU'LL NEED:
- Natural loose parts
- Nontoxic paints
- Painting tray or paper plates
- Paper

Continued on page 104

THE PROCESS:

Head outside to go on a nature walk with your little learner. Look for leaves and flowers of all shapes and sizes that would make interesting paintbrushes.

Add some natural paint colors to a tray—think about using different tones of greens, browns, oranges, reds, and yellows. Add your natural loose parts ready for your little learner to explore. They can dip their branches and flowers straight into the paint and experiment with making marks using their natural loose parts as brushes.

The artworks would look fantastic mounted on colored cardboard and displayed in your play space!

EXTEND IT

Are there any other objects in your home that you could use to make prints with? Try cutting interesting shapes into a potato to use as a stamper or using cooked spaghetti to make marks on a sheet of cardboard!

SPICE PAINTS

Add the sense of smell to your next painting experience with these scented spice paints! Your little learners will love exploring new smells while they create!

WHAT YOU'LL NEED:

- Nontoxic paints
- Paint palette
- Various spices
- Paintbrushes
- Paper

THE PROCESS:

Add some earthy colored paints to paint palette and add a generous sprinkle of each spice to the different-colored paints. For example, you might add some turmeric to a red, earthy color or some cinnamon to your brown paint.

These paints will smell absolutely amazing as your little learner creates with them. They'll also feel bumpy as they dry!

EXTEND IT:

Your little learner could add an extra sensory element to their artwork by gluing flowers and fresh herbs to their creation! Pressing flowers and leaves between two heavy books will make beautiful additions to any artwork.

SEED ROLLING

Your little learner will love using large arm movements to create a beautiful, marbled artwork using the seeds from their favorite fruits!

WHAT YOU'LL NEED:

- Large seeds from your favorite fruits (like an avocado)
- Paper
- A shallow painting tub
- Nontoxic paints

THE PROCESS:

Save the seed from an avocado to use for this creative sensory artwork! Add a piece of paper to the bottom of a shallow tub and then squirt a few drops of colored paint directly onto the paper. I like to use primary colors like yellow and blue or red and blue, not only because they mix nicely together, but also because they give our little learners a chance to explore color mixing.

Invite your little learner to drop their seed into the paint and then use large arm movements to shake the tub, moving the seed through the paint as they shake the tub from side to side.

The result is a beautifully marbled artwork that would look amazing displayed in your home!

EXTEND IT

Try creating a marbled artwork with smaller balls like marbles! You could even use balls of different sizes in the one tub to see how their finished artwork differs.

CLAY SCULPTURES

While manipulating and creating with clay, your little learner will be able to develop their hand and finger muscles. Your little learner will love creating their very own clay sculptures using natural loose parts from the garden.

WHAT YOU'LL NEED:
- Natural loose parts
- Matchsticks, cotton tips, and icy pole sticks
- Air-drying clay
- Nontoxic paints
- Googly eyes
- Craft glue

THE PROCESS:
Go on a nature walk together to collect some natural loose parts from the garden. Things like sticks, fallen leaves, feathers, and flowers all make wonderful additions to your clay sculptures.

You can also add things like matchsticks, icy pole sticks, and googly eyes in a sectioned tray. Have a ball of clay and some tools like rolling pins ready for your little learner to create!

EXTEND IT

Invite your little learner to create some insects from their clay. You can use a metal spoon to carve out and mold the body and then use natural loose parts to create their legs, wings, and antennae. They can then paint their creations once they're dry.

MIRROR PAINTING

Mirrors provide a great canvas for painting, as your little learner can explore mark-making from an entirely different perspective! The reflection also teaches young children about self-awareness.

WHAT YOU'LL NEED:
- Acrylic mirrors
- Nontoxic paints
- Brushes
- Paper

THE PROCESS:
You can either find an old mirror from a thrift shop or purchase flexible, acrylic mirrors, which are child-safe, from many home improvement stores or dollar shops.

Simply set out some paints and brushes and invite your little learner to explore the different canvas. We love to do this activity outside so that the clouds and trees are reflected in their mirrors as our little learners create.

Once they've finished exploring, place a piece of paper down onto the mirror and press down gently to make a print. You'll be able to keep their artwork forever!

EXTEND IT:

Add mirrors and fresh flowers to your art space and encourage your little learner to view the flowers from a new perspective. What can they see that they couldn't see before?

Final Notes

I hope you've found lots of inspiration to support you in getting started with sensory play throughout this book!

When I became a mother for the first time, I searched high and low for materials to support me in playing and learning with my baby. But I couldn't find the perfect resource that aligned with my beliefs of how children learn, especially in the early years. I eventually found myself creating countless sensory play tubs and realized quickly that sensory play was the answer! Not only did it allow me to support the developmental needs of my daughter, but it was also a lot of fun! I have such fond memories of her toddlerhood years filled with rainbow rice, finger painting, and edible small worlds.

We all want the very best for our little learners, but sometimes it can be so overwhelming not knowing where to start or what to do to support our children in their lifelong learning journey. This book came together to fill that need—to support other parents and educators who want to get started with sensory play but aren't sure how.

I cannot wait to hear how you use sensory play with your little learners! Don't forget to find me over on Instagram and share your photos so I can see all the playful memories you create together.

Happy playful learning!
Casey

About the Author

Casey Patch is an advocate for play-based learning in the early years. She has a bachelor's in primary education and was a classroom teacher before deciding to stay at home full-time after the birth of her first child. Creating a beautiful bond and magical memories of childhood during playtime is a passion of hers and one that she hopes to spread through her website and social media channels!

Casey lives in Brisbane, Australia, with her husband, Kurtis, who is also a stay-at-home parent. Together, they have three energetic children—Lilly, Elliot, and Audrey.

Over her years as a stay-at-home parent and educator, Casey has prepared hundreds of invitations to play. While sensory play is where her passion for playful learning began, she

also loves creating themed dramatic play spaces, preparing purposeful small worlds, facilitating process art explorations, and going on outdoor adventures with her own little learners.

Through her business, Little Lifelong Learners, Casey supports other parents to inject more play into their day. To find more playful inspiration for you and your little learners, head to www.littlelifelonglearners.com today!

Index

A
animal figurines, 7
artwork, sensory, 97–98

B
bath, color, 44–45
bath paints, 101–102
bird seed pouring tub, 47
bubble wrap painting, 95–96
bubbly soap foam, 33
building blocks, frozen, 61

C
chickpea foam, 27
chickpeas, rainbow, 14–15
clay sculptures, 108–109
clean up, 5
cloud dough, 18–19
color bath, 44–45
colorful explosions, 89–91

D
dirt dough, 21
dough
    cloud, 18–19
    dirt, 21
    play, 39–41

F
fizzy fish, 85
flower soup, 51
foam
    bubbly soap, 33
    chickpea, 27
    sandy, 25
frozen building blocks, 61
frozen nature blocks, 83–84
frozen oobleck blocks, 71–73
frozen water beads, 57–59

I
ice painting, 99–100

J
Jell-O bug rescue, 77–78

K
kitchen, 6
    outdoor, 74–75

L
language skills, 2
lavender sensory tub, 55–56
lemon tray, 48–49
life skills, 2

M
memory making, 3
mess, 5
mirror painting, 110–111
mud, edible, 22–23

N
nature blocks, frozen, 83–84
nature's paintbrushes, 103–104

O
ocean small world, 62
oobleck, 28–29
oobleck blocks, 71–73
oral language skills, 2
outdoor kitchen, 74–75

P
paintbrushes, nature's, 103–104
painting
    bubble wrap, 95–96
    ice, 99–100
    mirror, 110–111
paints
    bath, 101–102
    spice, 105
pantry, 6
play dough, 39–41
play dough small worlds, 52–53
polenta construction tub, 79–81

R
rainbow chickpeas, 14–15
rainbow rice, 11–13
rainbow spaghetti, 17
rice, rainbow, 11–13

S
sand foam, 25
sculptures, clay, 108–109
seed rolling, 106–107
sensory artwork, 97–98
sensory play
    benefits of, 1–2
    defining, 1–7
    staples, 6–7
simplicity, 5
small worlds
    edible ocean, 62
    play dough, 52–53
spaghetti, rainbow, 17
spice paints, 105
sticky wall, 64–65
supervision, 5

T
tub, 6
    bird seed pouring, 47
    lavender sensory, 55–56
    polenta construction, 79–81

W
wash the pigs, 67–68
water beads
edible, 30–31
    frozen, 57–59
water tub, 33–37